Beyond The Trees!
A kid's Guide to Lake Tahoe, California, USA

Photography By John D. Weigand
Poetry By Penelope Dyan

Bellissima Publishing, LLC
Jamul, California
www.bellissimapublishing.com

copyright © 2012 by Penny D. Weigand

All rights reserved. No part of this book may be reproduced or transmitted in any form or by any means, electronic or mechanical, including photocopying, recording, or by any other means, or by any information or storage retrieval system, without permission from the publisher.

ISBN 978-1-61477-027-5
First Edition

*Nature does not hurry,
yet everything is accomplished.*

Lao Tzu

Introduction

At Lake Tahoe, California the landscape changes along with the beauty of nature. This is a fun place to hike, bike or simply take a walk. You can drive from place to place and explore all on your own. There are bridges to cross, waterfalls to see, and the largest alpine lake in the United States, Lake Tahoe in Emerald Bay State Park, a California state park preserving Lake Tahoe's Emerald Bay, a National Natural Landmark! When you go to this place, there is more than anyone could ever put into any single book. This is why award winning author, attorney and former teacher, Penelope Dyan, and photographer John D. Weigand NEVER show everything there is to see in their travel guides for kids. Dyan believes imagination and adventure go together, and so these books look through the eyes of a child and see what a child sees--NO spoon-fed facts here! These books have very large print that a child can see the words easily as little eyes begin to read. The repetition, rhyme and humor all contribute to the process of learning. This is a book a child can make his or her own. Older children should write in the margins, take notes on what they see, and also insert their own photographs and drawings. No, there aren't any envelopes or flaps to stuff; and there are no "fill in the blanks." This would destroy the book's purpose. The purpose is to learn to think.

Beyond The Trees!
A Kid's Guide to Lake Tahoe, California, USA

Photography By John D. Weigand
Poetry By Penelope Dyan

Right there beyond the trees,
out there with the birds, bears and the bees,
a beautiful lake reaches right up to the sky,
framed by granite mountains reaching up so high.

The sun through the sky
promises the fall of snow,
and this is the place where
everyone will go.
Once the snow hits the ground,
people will come
from all around.
They will ski, and they will play,
but it appears the sun
is out today.

You give a tree by a cabin
a great big hug.
On the ground you see a bug.

On a paved walkway
you follow a path.
You skip and dance.
You sing and you laugh!

You see a park bench.
You see tree roots growing right out of the ground!
Everything is quiet.
There isn't a sound.

There are trees growing out of the mountain rock!
You and your parents stop and you talk.
You talk about nature sweet.
You tell them your new boots are hurting your feet!

There is a bridge that goes over a steam.
You keep on walking.
(After all, you're a team!)

Steps of stone and timber
go up high.
You tell your mom
your feet hurt.
She says, "Just give it a try!"

There are frozen waterfalls
(the Eagle Waterfalls)
and a great big bridge,
that you find once you climb
over the ridge.

The sky is still blue beyond the trees.
You complain the pain in your feet has now reached your knees!

You see Fannette Island.
There's a kind of castle on top!
You finally get to rest.
And so you all stop.
The water of Lake Tahoe is clear, beautiful and deep.
But it's been a long day and you just want to sleep.

And so you finally go back
to your hotel.
You take off your boots.
And all is well!

"Nature is the art of God."

-Ralph Waldo Emerson